To Rob and Paul, for putting up with the monkey business

Gorilla Doctors

SAVING ENDANGERED GREAT APES

Pamela S. Turner

Clarion Books
An Imprint of HarperCollinsPublishers
Boston New York

Mararo's "Jewelry"

Mararo is in trouble.

A nylon rope is looped tightly around her ankle and tied to a stake in the ground. A poacher set the snare to catch an antelope. Instead, it has snagged curious Mararo, a five-year-old mountain gorilla.

Agashya knows something is wrong. He is the silverback of Mararo's gorilla group, their leader, their protector. When Agashya hears a group of tourists and their guide coming through the forest, he defends helpless Mararo. Agashya roars, he screams, he shreds the forest, and he charges the invaders.

It isn't easy to face a rampaging four-hundred-pound gorilla, but Rwandan park guide Patience

ABOVE: Mike and Felicia prepare a dart to tranquilize Mararo. The dart has two chambers: one is filled with a drug to make her sleep, the other with compressed air. The air will inject the drug into Mararo.

PREVIOUS SPREAD: Silverback gorillas will fight to protect their families.

Dusabimana knows these animals well. He knows Agashya's tantrum is a warning, not an attack. Patience calmly moves the tourists away. As other park workers distract Agashya, Patience slashes the rope holding Mararo. But the loop is still wrapped around her ankle. Untreated, it may become infected. Mararo may lose her foot, or her life. Mararo needs the gorilla doctors.

The warden of Rwanda's Parc National des Volcans, where Mararo and her family live, calls Dr. Mike Cranfield and Dr. Felicia Nutter. Mike is the director of the Mountain Gorilla Veterinary Project (MGVP). Felicia is the MGVP's field veterinarian in Rwanda. At the park entrance, gorilla trackers, guides, and porters (who help carry equipment) join Mike and Felicia.

The team finds Agashya's group, but the gorillas are hard to follow. The nervous silverback keeps his nine-member family moving through the thick, wet forest. The gorillas easily cross deep, vine-tangled ravines by "knuckle walking" on all fours. But for the MGVP team, it is like struggling up and down slippery green staircases—with tripwires!

At last, Mararo stops for a snack of wild celery. Felicia's dart gun makes a soft "pffft" sound as she shoots a tranquilizer into Mararo's thigh. Mararo grunts, pulls out the dart, and walks away. But soon she is sleepy and topples over, face-down.

Agashya sits down next to Mararo. He eyes the humans warily. Mike, Felicia, and their team form a human "wall" and walk slowly toward the silverback. Agashya stands up and screams, then races off. His family follows.

Felicia, holding the
dart gun behind
her back, waits for
the right moment to
tranquilize Mararo.

ABOVE, LEFT AND RIGHT: Felicia and Rwandan park veterinary technician Elisabeth Nyirakaragire put a pulse oximeter on Mararo's lip. The yellow box next to Felicia shows how fast Mararo's heart is beating and how much oxygen is in her blood.

FACING PAGE: Felicia removes the snare from Mararo's ankle. Mountain gorillas are always treated in the forest. It is less stressful for the gorillas.

Mararo, though, doesn't move. Mike and Felicia quickly turn her over. Is the tranquilizer working properly? They clip a pulse oximeter to her lip. By measuring the amount of oxygen in Mararo's blood, the oximeter tells the vets that Mararo's heart and lungs are fine.

Felicia carefully removes the snare from Mararo's ankle. She recalls how Mararo needed another snare removed from her wrist the year before. "She must think they're jewelry," jokes Felicia. "I hope she doesn't find a third!"

Mike picks up Mararo's feet and compares them. The foot caught in the snare is only slightly swollen. Mararo will be fine.

Mike and Felicia measure Mararo and take samples of her blood, feces (poop), skin,

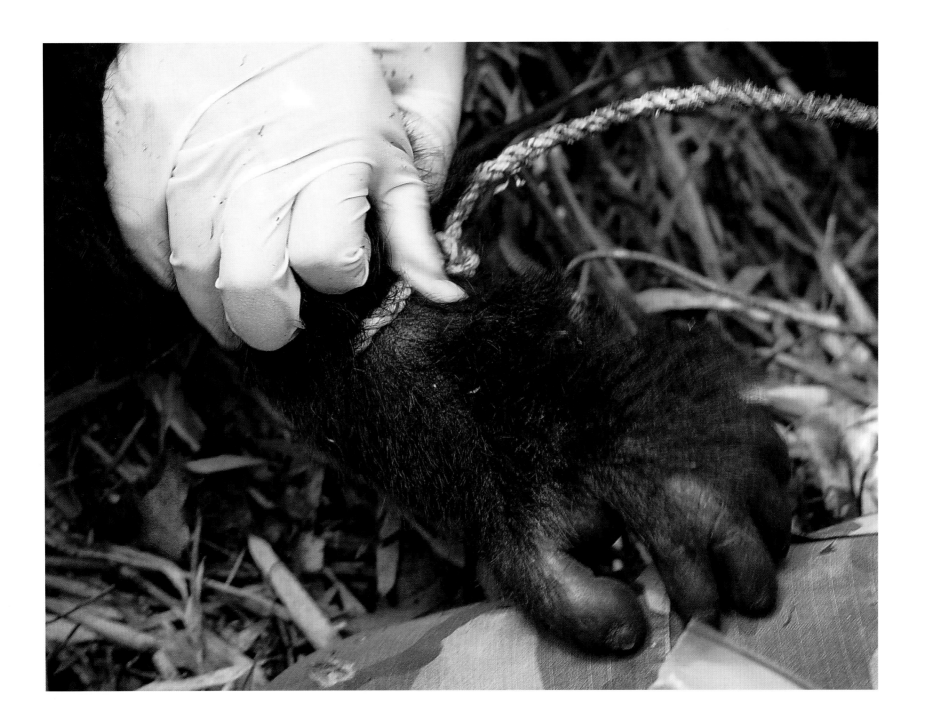

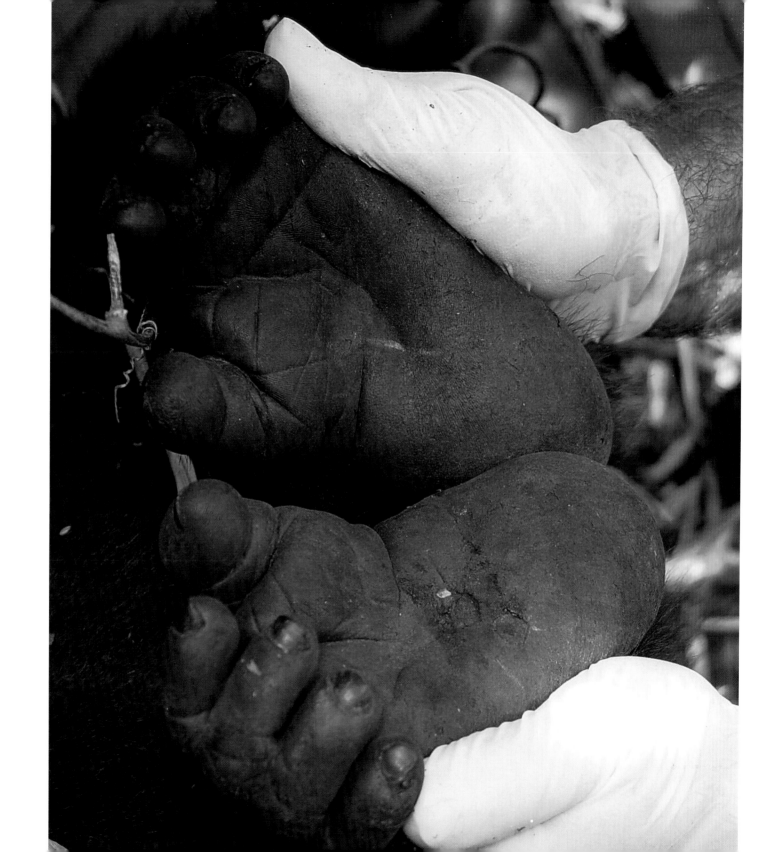

Mike compares Mararo's feet.

and hair. The blood will be tested to detect health problems such as liver and kidney disease. The fecal sample will be tested for internal parasites that may affect Mararo's health. The skin sample will be examined for external parasites like mites or ticks. A DNA analysis of Mararo's hair will help scientists understand how Mararo is related to other mountain gorillas.

Mararo begins to awaken. Her family has disappeared, but they left behind a "gorilla trail" of flattened plants. The MGVP team carries Mararo along the slippery trail in a small tarp. When she tries to sit up, they set her down. But groggy Mararo heads the wrong way. Mike, Felicia, and the rest of the team surround Mararo and gently herd her in the right direction. It takes hours, but finally Mararo's family hears her hooting and

ABOVE LEFT: Felicia measures Mararo while waiting for the tranquilizer to wear off. Everyone wears masks and gloves to prevent diseases from passing between the humans and the gorillas.

ABOVE RIGHT: As Mararo begins to wake up, she is carried back toward her gorilla family.

whimpering. They rush back. Mararo is reunited with Agashya and the rest of the group.

Mike and Felicia are happy that Mararo wasn't permanently injured. But sometimes other gorillas aren't so lucky. Two-year-old Karema, who joined Agashya's group with his mother earlier in the year, has no left hand, probably the result of an infected snare wound.

But snares set by poachers aren't the only danger facing these rare mountain gorillas. The MGVP scientists worry about a new threat just as deadly as a poacher but much harder to see: human disease.

Gorilla guide Patience Dusabimana with illegal snares collected in the park. The snares are usually set to catch small antelope, but sometimes the snares catch gorillas instead.

Scientists in the Mist

Hundreds of years ago, mountain gorillas weren't seriously threatened by human diseases, snares, spears, or guns. Thousands of mountain gorillas lived in the cool upland forests of east-central Africa. But bit by bit, acre by acre, farmers cut down the forests for farmland. Mountain gorillas were pushed higher and higher up the mountain slopes.

Scientists didn't know about mountain gorillas until 1902, when German officer Robert von Beringe shot two in the Virunga Mountains. The mountain gorilla's scientific name is *Gorilla beringei beringei,* after von Beringe.

ABOVE: One of the five mountain gorillas killed during the 1921 Akeley expedition

FACING PAGE: George Schaller records his gorilla observations at his cabin in the Virungas in 1959. Schaller was the first scientist to study wild gorillas. He also pioneered field studies of tigers, lions, snow leopards, and pandas.

In 1921, the American hunter Carl Akeley traveled to the Virungas to collect mountain gorilla specimens for New York's American Museum of Natural History. Akeley had read that gorillas were "hellish creatures." But when he looked into the face of a freshly shot silverback, Akeley felt not triumph but shame:

> As he lay at the base of the tree, it took all one's scientific ardor to keep from feeling like a murderer. He was a magnificent creature with the face of an amiable giant who would do no harm except perhaps in self-defense or in defense of his friends.

Akeley went to the Belgian government, which in those days controlled the Virungas. He persuaded them to create Albert National Park to protect the gorillas from hunters. Founded in 1925, it was the first national park in Africa. But calling an area a park isn't enough to protect its wildlife.

George Schaller was the first scientist to study wild gorillas. He spent twenty months during 1959–60 in the Virungas. To study the mountain gorillas, he needed to get close to them. As the scientist followed the gorillas from a distance and then shortened the distance bit by bit, the animals gradually got used to him. The process is called *habituation*. Schaller watched what the gorillas ate, how they treated one another, and where they traveled. He listened to the sounds they made. He learned that they spent most of their day munching plants, playing, and resting. Although adult males sometimes fought, they preferred bluffing to biting.

RIGHT: When Peanuts patted Dian Fossey's hand in 1970, it was the first time a wild gorilla had ever voluntarily touched a human. People are no longer allowed to get this close, except for veterinarians treating injured gorillas.

FACING PAGE: The Virungas are a chain of volcanoes. Mountain gorillas live in the misty forests that cover the steep slopes. Mountain gorillas have long, thick hair to keep them warm in this cool, rainy environment.

Seven years after Schaller left the Virungas, Dian Fossey arrived. She knew about Schaller's research and wanted to learn even more. The gorillas eventually became so used to Fossey that they allowed her to sit very close. One day, a wild gorilla named Peanuts reached out and touched her hand. Fossey was so happy she burst into tears.

Fossey soon realized that the gorillas and their park were threatened by poachers and by cattle grazing inside the park, so she hired guards to patrol it. They chased out

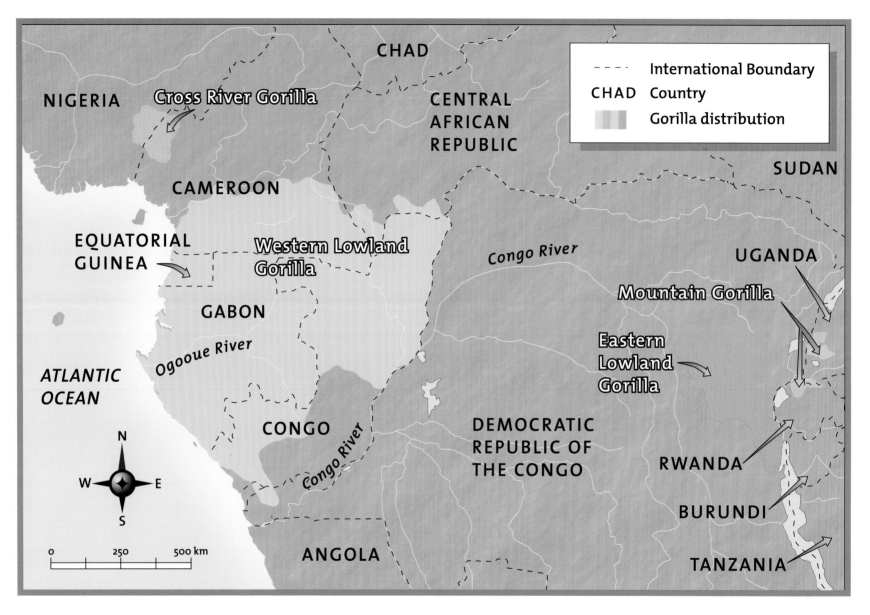

All gorillas live in Africa. There are two species: the western gorilla (*Gorilla gorilla*) and the eastern gorilla (*Gorilla beringei*). There are two gorilla subspecies in the west: the western lowland gorilla (*Gorilla gorilla gorilla*), and the very rare Cross River gorilla (*Gorilla gorilla diehli*). There are only about 150 to 200 Cross River gorillas. There are two gorilla subspecies in the east: the eastern lowland gorilla (*Gorilla beringei graueri*), and the mountain gorilla (*Gorilla beringei beringei*).

cattle, collected snares, and destroyed poacher camps. But the park was big, and the forest easy to hide in.

Gorillas continued to die. Some were killed so their heads and hands could be made into souvenirs. Others were killed to capture their babies for pets. And some were killed or injured in snares set for other animals. In 1960, Schaller estimated that there were about 450 gorillas in the Virungas. By 1981, only about 250 were left.

In 1984, Ruth Keesling visited Dian Fossey in Rwanda. Fossey asked Keesling, whose father had founded Morris Animal Foundation to promote animal health, if a veterinary program could be set up to care for mountain gorillas harmed by humans. Keesling promised to help.

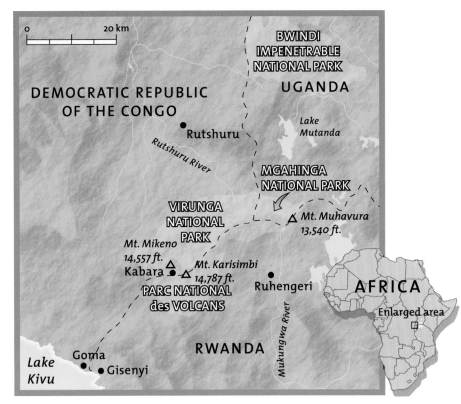

Mountain gorillas are found in two areas in east-central Africa. About half of all mountain gorillas live in the Virunga region, where the borders of Uganda, Rwanda, and the Democratic Republic of the Congo come together. The other half of the mountain gorilla population lives in Bwindi Impenetrable Forest in western Uganda.

Fossey believed veterinarians could help save mountain gorillas from extinction. There were so few gorillas left, every single one was important. A vet might have saved gorillas like Mweza and Lee, who died when their snare injuries became infected. Little Kweli, shot in the arm by a poacher, might also have lived if his wound had been properly treated.

Fossey had also worried about the deaths of two other gorillas, Nunkie and Charles Darwin. Human doctors examined the gorillas after their mysterious deaths and found that both were infested with hookworms, an intestinal parasite. Fossey knew that many humans in the Virungas also suffered from hookworms. She realized that the gorillas might be dying not just from bullets, spears, or snares, but also from diseases that might have come from humans. And diseases from humans couldn't be blamed just

on poachers. Human diseases could be spread by park workers, tourists, or researchers like Fossey. "Maybe poachers aren't the worst thing to happen to gorillas," wrote Fossey. "Perhaps WE are."

The following year, Fossey was murdered at her research station in the Virungas. No one knows who killed her, but many people think she was murdered by someone who did not like her fierce efforts to protect gorillas. Fossey was buried next to her favorite gorilla, Digit. Digit had been killed by poachers seven years earlier.

Six months after Fossey's death, the first MGVP veterinarian arrived in Rwanda. MGVP (funded by the Morris Animal Foundation) was the first veterinary service to care for an endangered animal in its natural environment. There was still hope for the mountain gorillas.

FACING PAGE: Gorillas are mostly vegetarians, though they sometimes eat ants and grubs. Mountain gorillas' favorite foods are bamboo shoots, bramble, wild celery, nettles, and thistles.

ABOVE: The lord and master of a gorilla family is the silverback, an adult male. The hair on a male's back turns silver as he matures. Adult male mountain gorillas can reach 450 pounds (205 kilograms). They are the largest of all great apes.

Our Closest Kin

Felicia's throbbing foot was propped on a pillow. She had

broken it two days before while walking down some stairs. It was the worst possible time for a gorilla to get sick.

The warden of Rwanda's Parc National des Volcans called. "Agashya's not well. You need to take a look," he told her, describing the gorilla's cough.

Felicia had been told to stay off her foot for six weeks. But gorilla doctors make house calls — or rather, forest calls. The next day Felicia was limping up a volcano on crutches. "It was a slippery, steep hike," says Felicia. "A five-hour crawl up the mountain."

An exhausted Felicia finally reached Agashya. To her relief, Agashya wasn't coughing much and was very alert. "He grumbled when he saw me," says Felicia. Felicia watched for signs of illness in the rest of Agashya's group. One female was coughing, but otherwise the group looked healthy.

Luckily, Agashya recovered without needing any treatment. But Felicia had good reason to be worried about him. Just a few months before, two gorillas in another group had died from pneumonia. "One gorilla had the worst case I have ever seen," says Felicia. "We don't know if the disease was transmitted from humans, but it is possible."

How could a gorilla catch a human disease? Diseases pass most easily between species when the species are close biologically and come into close contact with each other.

Biologically, we are very close to great apes — so close that we share 98.4 percent of our genes with chimpanzees and bonobos (sometimes called "pygmy chimpanzees") and 97.7 percent

LEFT: Mother gorillas nurse their babies for about eighteen months. Baby gorillas are only about four and a half pounds (two kilograms) at birth, but they develop about twice as fast as human babies.

PREVIOUS SPREAD: Adult male silverbacks like Agashya can eat sixty pounds (twenty-seven kilograms) of plants a day. You can see where it ends up—in his big potbelly.

of our genes with gorillas. So close that a chimpanzee or a bonobo could give you a blood transfusion — or you could give blood to them. And the closer two species are, the easier it is for them to have common diseases.

Organisms that cause infectious disease are called *pathogens*. Pathogens can be viruses (like AIDS or the common cold), bacteria (like salmonella or tuberculosis), fungi (like ringworm or athlete's foot), or parasites (like scabies and hookworm). Pathogens are adapted to certain "host" species, just as a polar bear is adapted to the Arctic or a cactus to the desert. If a new host is similar to the old one, a pathogen can more easily adapt to the new host.

Great Ape and Human Populations: How's the Family?

THE HIGHER PRIMATES	ESTIMATED POPULATION (2004)
Human	6,396,000,000
Chimpanzee	200,000
Bonobo	15,000
Orangutan	53,500
Gorilla	100,000
Mountain Gorilla (SUBSPECIES)	700

There are fewer mountain gorillas in the world than there are students at the average American middle school.

Disease can pass between less closely related species, too. You've probably heard of measles, tuberculosis, smallpox, whooping cough, and the flu. Human diseases, right? Actually, all originated in domestic animals. Measles, tuberculosis, and smallpox came from cattle; whooping cough from pigs and dogs; and flu from pigs and ducks.

How does this happen? Just as animals can adapt over time to changes in their environment, a pathogen can adapt over time to a new host. People have been in close contact with domestic animals like cattle, pigs, and dogs for thousands of years. Some

ABOVE: Gorillas get runny noses, too! Scientists believe many diseases, including the common cold, can pass between humans and gorillas.

FACING PAGE: A young gorilla gives her shoulder a scratch. When you watch a gorilla you can't help but notice how human they seem—or perhaps how gorilla-like *we* seem!

of these animals' pathogens adapted to humans. Many pathogens can evolve into new forms quickly because they reproduce quickly. A virus may go through several hundred generations in a single year.

Pathogens are still "jumping" from species to species. Scientists think that the virus that causes AIDS originated in chimpanzees and infected humans when a chimp was butchered and eaten. Other new human diseases with animal origins are SARS, Ebola, West Nile virus, Lyme disease, Nipah virus, and new types of bird flu.

Over time, a host can become resistant to a disease. Many hosts may die, but the surviving hosts pass their resistance to their offspring. Resistance builds up in a population and fewer hosts die. But if the disease infects a new species or population without any resistance, the results can be devastating.

When Europeans came to the Americas they brought along terrible diseases like measles and smallpox that were new to Native Americans. Native Americans had never been exposed to these diseases and had little resistance. In some places 95 percent of the people perished. In the same way, gorillas have little resistance to new diseases they catch from humans.

Of course, wild gorillas try to stay far away from people. But as the human population grows, fewer places are truly remote. And habituation (wild animals' becoming gradually accustomed to humans) can add to the problem. Habituated gorillas provide scientists with important information, and tourist visits to habituated gorillas generate

money that can be used for conservation. But habituation also brings gorillas closer than ever to people and their pathogens.

In 1988, a strange disease struck mountain gorillas in Rwanda. They coughed and had difficulty breathing. Their noses ran. The gorillas huddled in their nests all day, too sick to eat. Six gorillas died. All of the sick gorillas belonged to habituated groups regularly visited by people.

MGVP veterinarians examined the dead gorillas. They found evidence of measles in tissue and blood samples, which suggested why so many gorillas got sick and died. The gorillas would have had little resistance to this human disease.

Should the remaining gorillas be given a human measles vaccine? There was a risk. No one had ever tried to vaccinate wild gorillas before. But if MGVP did nothing, the Virunga's mountain gorillas might be wiped out.

Scientists believe chimpanzees have died from human diseases like polio, scabies, influenza, and pneumonia.

Deadly Neighbors

Great apes in the wild are threatened by human diseases, as well as by habitat loss and poaching. Other wild animals are also vulnerable to the diseases of people, their pets, and livestock. Here are just a few examples:

WILD SPECIES	DISEASE	WHERE THE DISEASE COMES FROM	HOW DO SCIENTISTS THINK THE WILD ANIMALS GET THE DISEASE?
Lions, hyenas, African wild dogs, bat-eared foxes, and leopards in Tanzania	Canine distemper virus	Domestic dogs	Hyenas and village dogs come into contact while scavenging in village garbage dumps; hyenas bring the virus back into the park, where it spreads at kill sites visited by other predators
Sea otters off the central California coast	*Toxoplasma gondii*, a parasite, causes brain infection	Domestic cats	Cat feces containing parasite eggs are washed into the ocean, where otters get them from the water or by eating infected shellfish
Iberian lynxes, the world's rarest cat, in Spain	Bovine tuberculosis	Domestic cattle	Domestic cattle infect wild deer and boar; lynxes get the disease when they feed on deer and boar
Ethiopian wolves, the world's rarest dog, in Ethiopia	Rabies	Domestic dogs	Dogs follow people bringing livestock to graze in wolf habitat
Meerkats and banded mongooses in Botswana	Human tuberculosis	Humans	Meerkats and mongooses touch infected items while scavenging through village garbage dumps or along roadsides

Sixty-five gorillas were vaccinated with a dart gun. Thankfully, the vaccine seemed to work. None of the vaccinated gorillas became sick, and the infections stopped. It was now clear to MGVP scientists that human disease could threaten the gorillas' survival. But understanding the link between gorilla health and human health would take a lot of something scientists always need—data.

Canine distemper threatens lions, hyenas, and other predators in the Serengeti. The 30,000 domestic dogs living in villages around the park now get regular distemper and rabies vaccinations. Although people can't get distemper from dogs, they can get rabies. The vaccinations mean better health for both people and animals.

Out of the Forest

On a small Ugandan farm, a boy tends his family's bean crop. Running alongside the farm is a wall of greenery—the border of the Bwindi Impenetrable Forest. It takes a lot of work with hoe and machete to keep the forest from swallowing the family's crops.

The boy puts on his blue uniform and walks down the red dirt road to school. That afternoon, a gorilla group strolls out of the forest and gathers at the edge of the farm. The gorillas like the sunny clearings made by farmers. Nkuringo, the silverback, has led his family here for a gorilla's favorite afternoon—eating, playing, and relaxing.

The boy's farm has a grove of banana plants. This looks very tasty to Nkuringo. He ambles over to a banana plant and tears long strips off the trunk. Nkuringo ignores the ripening fruit. Mountain gorillas prefer the soft inside of the banana plant's trunk. Soon other gorillas join in—Faida, Rafiki, Christmas, Safari, Bahati, and Samehe, clutching her newborn baby. When the gorillas return to the forest, several banana trees look as if they've been hit by a hurricane.

The next morning, MGVP scientists Dr. Mike Cranfield, Dr. Innocent Rwego, and Dr. Lynne Gaffikin walk past the boy's farm. The three are here to gather data on the health of mountain gorillas.

Innocent, Mike, and Lynne scramble down a hillside, grabbing vines and dead branches while keeping an eye out for stinging nettles. The gorilla tracker points to some bulky black shapes moving across a hillside: Nkuringo and his family. They've left the farm and are heading back to the forest.

Half of the world's mountain gorillas live here in the Bwindi Impenetrable Forest. Some gorilla groups in both Bwindi and the Virungas are habituated so tourists can visit them. The Nkuringo group is supposed to be visited by tourists, but the Ugandan government's first concern is the gorillas' health. Not long ago, Innocent treated many of these gorillas for scabies—a disease the gorillas probably got from people.

Scabies, a common skin problem in this part of Africa, is caused by tiny mites that burrow under the skin. Scabies is annoying, like a poison oak rash, but it isn't a serious disease — at least not in humans. However, scabies can be life-threatening to gorillas, especially young ones. In 1996 a baby mountain gorilla in Bwindi died from a skin disease veterinarians believe was scabies. The baby lost most of its hair and became so weak it could no longer cling to its mother.

In 2000, some of Nkuringo's group were scratching themselves and losing patches of hair. Mike hiked down into a valley to examine and treat the gorillas. He anesthetized the sick gorillas and gave them injections of medicine that makes the skin poisonous to mites. "After several hours the two adult males in the group got tired of us, and they charged from two different directions. I'll never forget *that* feeling!" recalls Mike. "You're never supposed to run, but it was all I could do to just sit there."

As the Baltimore Zoo's head veterinarian, Mike has treated a Noah's Ark of animals. One of his oddest tasks was to remove porcupine quills — from a porcupine! "Two porcupines got in a fight, and one got a taste of its own medicine," explains Mike.

While dodging charging silverbacks, Mike took small samples from the gorillas' bald patches and sent them to a laboratory. Scientists confirmed that the mountain gorillas were infested with the same mite that causes scabies in humans.

Scabies hit Nkuringo's family again last year. Innocent used the dart gun to give four gorillas medicine, and they all recovered.

ABOVE: This baby mountain gorilla lost most of its hair and died after catching scabies.

FACING PAGE: Innocent, Lynne, and Mike field-test a PDA in Uganda.

"The mountain gorillas often leave the forest and forage in people's gardens," says Innocent. "Many people use a corner of their garden as a garbage dump, and curious gorillas will sometimes pick up things they find in there. We think gorillas get scabies from handling old clothes. Then scabies spreads from gorilla to gorilla."

Innocent is the MGVP veterinarian in Uganda. He grew up on a farm not far from Bwindi. His grandfather kept a small herd of cattle, but they all died, one by one. "I decided that I would become a vet because my grandfather depended on those cattle, and to see them die hurt very much," says Innocent.

Innocent, Mike, and Lynne find Nkuringo's group. They walk slowly toward the gorillas, trying to spot as many as they can in the thick brush. Mike pulls out a PDA (short for "personal digital assistant"), a hand-held minicomputer. The PDA data are later downloaded into a computer for analysis.

"The gorilla trackers see these gorillas every day and can recognize each one by sight," explains Lynne. "The trackers use either a paper form or the PDA. They start with a gorilla 'roll call.' Is each gorilla here? Is the gorilla scratching? Is it coughing? Does it have a runny nose? We're looking for early signs of health problems, like infected wounds, scabies, intestinal parasites, and pneumonia, so the vets can be alerted right away. But we're also gathering data that will answer questions about the health of all the gorillas."

Lynne is MGVP's epidemiologist. Veterinarians and medical doctors usually focus on curing individual patients. Epidemiologists are interested in health, too, but their main goal is to understand health problems in a *population* rather than in an individual. What diseases appear in the population? Which individuals in the population are getting sick? How is the disease spreading from one individual to another or from one population to another?

FACING PAGE: Farmland surrounds Bwindi Impenetrable Forest in Uganda. A local group called HUGO (for HUman-GOrilla) tries to herd the gorillas back into the park when they come too close to farmers' crops.

A young female member of Nkuringo's group, Bahati, feeding in Bwindi. Female mountain gorillas weigh from 150 to 250 pounds (from 68 to 114 kilograms). They are able to have babies at about age seven.

The health of different populations living near each other is often linked. Lynne and the other MGVP scientists suspect that the health of the gorillas is linked to the health of the people living around the parks.

"When one gorilla gets a disease, it doesn't tell us a lot. But data on all the gorillas, put together, can help us see patterns," says Lynne. "Over time, PDA data can help us answer questions like, Are gorillas that spend most of their time near farms more likely to get scabies than gorillas that stay inside the park? The answer can help us find ways of protecting the gorillas from disease."

Lynne has always been interested in apes and monkeys. Her father, an actor, once played a gorilla in a movie. "I guess it's in my blood," she jokes.

Bahati, a young female gorilla, sits down to feed in sight of Innocent, Mike, and Lynne. Faida comes by, too. Faida is a blackback—a young male who doesn't yet have the silver hair that will mark his maturity. Faida may one day take over from the silverback Nkuringo, or leave the group to start his own group. Both Bahati and Faida get high health marks. Mike puts the information into the PDA.

All of the world's mountain gorillas live in two "islands" of parkland surrounded by a sea of people. There are no mountain gorillas in captivity.

Gorillas are smart and curious. A young gorilla has found a juicy red fruit. It is too bitter to eat, but it makes a wonderful toy. The young gorilla shows it to a smaller playmate. Then she rubs the sticky pulp on her face and belly, just for fun!

Mike, Innocent, and Lynne circle around the group. It is hard to get a good look at each gorilla in the thick brush. They catch only a fleeting glimpse of the new mother Samehe. Samehe was one of the gorillas Innocent treated for scabies. Samehe seems fine now as she hugs a ball of black fluff against her chest. "It's a boy," the gorilla tracker says. "He's two months old, but he doesn't have a name yet."

The MGVP team heads back to the trackers' camp. The PDA test has gone well. It's time for a small celebration. Mike, Innocent, and Lynne buy a goat from a nearby farm. The MGVP team and the trackers will have a feast to celebrate naming the baby gorilla. But what to call Samehe's little bundle of joy?

Something fitting, something African. Finally, everyone settles on "Amagara." The name is a wish for all gorillas.

In the local Ugandan language, Amagara means "health."

A Game of Clue

Mike, Lynne, and Innocent follow the trail of Nkuringo

and his family. They aren't trying to find the gorillas, though. They are tracking backwards to find the gorillas' night nests.

A gorilla group follows a simple schedule, led by the silverback. The gorillas wake, find a nice eating spot, and then settle down for a midday rest. Afterward, the gorillas eat again. As the sun begins to set the silverback chooses a spot for the group to spend the night. Each gorilla (except youngsters, who sleep with their mothers) builds a night nest. The nest is a circle of flattened and bent plants. A new one is built every evening.

The night nests are very important to scientists. Only some mountain gorilla groups are habituated. Many other gorillas are still wild and keep their distance from people. But scientists can tell how many wild gorillas are in the forest by counting night nests. And because the gorillas usually defecate (poop) in their nests just before leaving, nests provide fecal samples for laboratory analysis.

Mike, Lynne, and Innocent hike over a small stream almost hidden by thick vines. There they are: giant saucers of twisted grass, the night nests of Nkuringo and his family. In each nest a gorilla has left a little contribution (sometimes a large contribution) to science.

One of the night nests contains loose feces. It could mean the gorilla is infected with diarrhea-causing bacteria. Other nests have normal-looking feces. Innocent and Lynne collect a sample of each. The samples will be tested for intestinal parasites like hookworms and diarrhea-causing bacteria. What comes *out* of the body can tell scientists what is going on *inside* the body.

LEFT: Innocent collects a fecal sample from a gorilla's night nest. Nests are usually built on the ground, but sometimes a youngster will build one in a tree or bush.

FACING PAGE: Baby gorillas stay very close to their mothers. At naptime and nighttime they cuddle in the same nest.

If there is a human disease that might harm the gorillas, identifying the disease is only the first step. The MGVP scientists also want to understand where it came from and how it reached the gorillas. It's like a scientific game of Clue — but instead of Miss Scarlet in the library with the candlestick, it might be bacteria in the forest from unburied human feces, or scabies mites in the farmers' fields from castoff clothing.

"It is very hard to 'prove' that gorillas are suffering from human diseases," says Lynne. "Once we identify a disease that might be coming from humans, we try to figure out how it could get to the gorillas. Then we can find ways to protect the gorillas from the disease."

A previous study found that the number of habituated gorillas with diarrhea-causing bacteria in their feces has increased over time. Some wild gorillas carry diarrhea-causing bacteria, too, but the bacteria are more common in habituated gorillas. One-hundred and twenty-eight fecal samples were collected to find this pattern.

How did the bacteria reach the gorillas? The MGVP scientists are checking fecal samples from other creatures that live in and around the park. They plan to test

ABOVE: The circle of flattened grass in front of Lynne is a gorilla's night nest. Lynne collects a fecal sample from the nest for laboratory analysis.

FACING PAGE: Felicia checks fecal samples for organisms that can make the gorillas sick.

humans, cattle, and other wildlife to see which carry the same diarrhea-causing bacteria.

Often the results of one study give clues about what research to do next. If gorillas do share a pathogen (like disease-causing bacteria) with other animals, the scientists will check to see if the pathogen appears in the same areas at the same time. They'll also do a DNA analysis to find out if the pathogen infecting the gorillas is really the same as the one found in other animals (many bacteria look alike). Next, they will try to find out how the pathogen spreads. Human or animal wastes left in the forest? Contaminated

ABOVE LEFT: Every year thousands of tourists visit the mountain gorillas. The tourists must follow strict rules that help prevent the gorillas from catching human diseases.

LEFT: Gorillas that are used to people sometimes come into farmer's fields. This can expose them to disease.

water? A scientist is never sure what he or she will discover—will it be an answer, a dead end, or will it lead to another intriguing question?

The MGVP scientists don't have all the answers. Luckily they don't need all the answers in order to help protect the gorillas.

"We started an employee health program in Rwanda to make sure that all the trackers and guides who work in the park get regular medical checkups," says Mike. "And we worked with the governments of Uganda, Rwanda, and the Democratic Republic of the Congo, along with other conservation groups, to come up with new rules for tourists."

Sick people are not allowed to enter the parks. The number of tourists is limited, and their visits can only be as long as one hour. Everyone must stay at least twenty-three feet (seven meters) from the gorillas. They aren't allowed to smoke or eat while

ABOVE: Lynne's son Joshua and her "pet apes" look on as Lynne analyzes gorilla health data at her home in Baltimore, Maryland.

ABOVE LEFT: Innocent and Felicia prepare, sort, and label fecal samples in MGVP's laboratory.

The Mountain Gorilla Veterinary Project is at the forefront of a new field called *conservation medicine.* Conservation medicine recognizes that wildlife health doesn't exist in a vacuum. The health of animals is related to the health of humans and the health of the environment. By understanding the transfer of disease between different species, and finding ways to control or prevent disease, conservation medicine hopes to make our planet healthier.

near the gorillas, and all garbage must be carried out of the park. All human waste must be buried.

Still, gorillas sometimes get hurt or become sick. MGVP vets are allowed to treat gorillas if the problem is life-threatening or caused by humans.

"Some people might say we should let the gorillas die 'natural' deaths and never treat them," says Mike. "But these gorillas live in parks surrounded on all sides by people. We've changed the risks the gorillas face. The least we can do is to help them whenever people are the source of the problem."

Why not just keep everyone away from gorillas? Gorilla tourism brings in a lot of money and encourages people to protect the animals. And just telling people not to enter the park wouldn't keep poachers out. The trackers and guides who enter the park with tourists help discourage poaching. But poaching still goes on, sometimes with tragic results.

The Fearless Orphan

The orphan gorilla arrived at Felicia's house late one night,

starved and scared. But when Felicia picked him up and made happy gorilla sounds, he clung to her with his skinny arms and cuddled against her chest.

His caretakers named him Ntabwoba, which means "fearless" in Rwandan. Fearless had been found earlier that day in a small village. Policemen arrested the poachers and brought Fearless to Felicia.

A gorilla group is very protective of its infants. To catch a baby, poachers often kill the silverback, other adult males in the group, and the baby's mother. Sometimes an entire gorilla family is killed to steal one

infant. Although killing gorillas and selling babies is illegal, some people are willing to risk jail because a baby gorilla is worth a lot of money. And some people want a pet gorilla as a "status symbol" and don't care about the terrible damage they are doing by buying these babies.

Because of his short fur, Felicia suspected that Fearless was not a mountain gorilla but an eastern lowland gorilla. A DNA analysis of Fearless's hair later proved Felicia right.

"As soon as I saw Fearless, I knew he was about nine or ten months old," says Felicia. "His mother would still be nursing him. He was covered in lice, very underweight, and had diarrhea. But he was remarkably bright and responsive, given everything he'd been through."

Felicia knew that a dehydrated infant can easily die. She needed to get something into Fearless — fast. She offered Fearless rehydration fluids (like a sports drink) in a bottle, but he refused. Felicia tried a large syringe (a tube with a plunger inside). Fearless took it happily.

Baby gorillas spend every moment of their lives in the warm embrace of their mother. Fearless needed fluids, but he needed comfort, too. Felicia took Fearless to bed, lice and all. "I was just hoping I wouldn't have to be deloused, too!" she says. "He wouldn't settle down and spent the whole night scratching. He had diarrhea. And he peed. It was a wet, messy night."

The next morning Fearless seemed better. Felicia mixed up a formula from cow's

Felicia decided to become a veterinarian when she was four. "I was always bringing home orphan birds and bunnies," says Felicia. "They often died. I wanted to learn how to fix them."

milk, eggs, and sugar, and added a medicine that made Fearless's skin poisonous to lice. "He really improved quickly," says Felicia.

Fearless is now doing well, but he still needs round-the-clock care. The warden of Rwanda's Parc National des Volcans sent people to help Felicia, as did the Karisoke Research Center (where Dian Fossey once studied gorillas). "Everyone obeys special rules," explains Felicia. "We don't want Fearless to catch any illnesses from his caregivers, or give them any diseases." Everyone who cares for Fearless must pass a health check. They wear special clothes and shower before and after they care for the baby gorilla.

Fearless spends most of the day in Felicia's large walled garden. Felicia carries out a cereal/milk/vitamin mixture and fresh papaya for Fearless's lunch. After eating, Fearless crawls into Felicia's lap. She hands him "toys": a peeled bamboo shoot and a little bouquet of purple flowers. Felicia collected these gorilla foods for Fearless. "In the wild, his mother would breastfeed him for eighteen months," explains Felicia. "But infant gorillas play with food they see their mothers eating. They learn a lot by watching."

Felicia picks up the purple flowers. "Gorillas eat this plant,

It is important for baby gorillas to play with their food. Many natural gorilla foods are prickly or have tough coverings. Through play, baby gorillas learn how to eat the plants they need to survive.

and it is also used by people when they have colds. Fearless has a slight runny nose, so this might help him. It is from nature's medicine chest."

After cuddling, Fearless explores the yard. Everything goes in his mouth, just as with a human baby. Fearless wanders over to a canna lily and pulls it to the ground. It is easy to imagine how Felicia's garden will look in a few months—flattened!

Fearless's future is uncertain. Reintroducing a gorilla back into the wild can be very difficult. Gorillas learn how to be a gorilla from other gorillas. Although Fearless's caregivers do their best to sound and act like gorillas, it is not the same.

ABOVE: Like a wild gorilla, Fearless gets twenty-four-hour care.

FACING PAGE: Felicia feeds Fearless with a syringe as he sits on Elisabeth Nyira-karagire's lap. As a veterinary technician with the Rwandan park service, Elisabeth has worked with mountain gorillas for thirteen years.

"The longer a gorilla stays in captivity, the harder it is to reintroduce it back into the wild," says Felicia. "But Fearless is so young, he will need to stay in captivity another three years or so before we could consider reintroducing him into the wild. And for Fearless, it might not even be an option."

Reintroduction is very difficult for male gorillas like Fearless. When a female gorilla grows up, she sometimes leaves her family group and joins another. Silverbacks are happy to accept adult females so they can mate with them. But unknown males are seen as competitors.

Fearless bounds across the lawn and pounces on Jean-Paul, one of his caretakers. Fearless bares his teeth just like a puppy as they wrestle in the grass. "Fearless really *is* absolutely fearless," says Felicia. "And vocal. He makes play sounds, food sounds, and laughs."

Fearless is incredibly cute. It's easy to imagine him in a zoo, amusing thousands of children with his playful antics. But Fearless is a gorilla, and gorillas are highly endangered animals. Fearless belongs in the forest, not in a backyard. He should be sleeping in a gorilla nest, not in a bed. Captive gorillas are lost forever to those who need them most: their fellow gorillas struggling to survive in the wild.

ABOVE LEFT AND RIGHT: In the wild, baby gorillas explore the forest under the watchful eyes of their mother. Fearless's "forest" is Felicia's garden.

FACING PAGE: Fearless likes to chew on things, just as a human baby does.

Jean-Paul Gahire plays with Fearless. Jean-Paul is a gorilla tracker with the Karisoke Research Center. When he is not caring for Fearless, he follows gorilla groups in the forest. He observes their behavior and helps protect them from poachers.

Gorillas in the Garden

Innocent stands in front of a seventh grade classroom.

"How many of you have seen a gorilla?" he asks.

The children look at each other, but nobody raises a hand.

"Can you tell me the dangers to gorillas?" asks Innocent.

"Poaching."

"Lack of security in the parks."

"Lack of pasture."

ABOVE LEFT AND RIGHT: Innocent returns to his old primary school to talk about mountain gorillas.

FACING PAGE: The MGVP scientists hike past farmers' fields to reach the mountain gorillas.

"Lack of water."

"Gorillas rarely, if ever, drink water," explains Innocent. "They get the water they need from the plants they eat. But poaching is a problem, people coming into the parks without permission is a problem. And the gorillas only have so much parkland."

This is Seseme Primary School in Kisoro, Uganda, twenty miles (thirty-two kilometers) from Bwindi Impenetrable Forest. Innocent knows this school well. He used to go to school here, though in those days Seseme was much smaller. Today there are 1,264 students and 28 teachers. Uganda's population has doubled in the last twenty years. The population of neighboring Rwanda has grown almost as quickly.

"Disease is also a problem for gorillas," Innocent tells the students. "They can

get diseases from us. Sometimes the gorillas cross the park boundary. If people sneeze on something, or throw away clothes with scabies mites in them, the gorillas can get sick. What can we do to prevent diseases from going to the gorillas from people, or diseases from gorillas to people?"

A girl suggests building latrines. (Many rural Ugandans do not have flush toilets.) "That is a good idea," says Innocent. "That keeps people healthy, too. And the government is buying land around the park to make a buffer zone between gorillas and people. And when people go into the park, like tourists or guides, they cannot get too close to gorillas. They cannot go into the park if they are sick."

Innocent tells them that foreigners pay $250 to spend just one hour watching gorillas. The students gasp. Then they laugh. (The average yearly income per person in Uganda and Rwanda is about $250. In the United States it is about $35,000.

Imagine if someone told you Ugandans paid $35,000 to spend an hour watching bison graze. You'd laugh, too!)

A boy raises his hand. "Some people say we shouldn't care so much about gorillas because they aren't as important as people."

Innocent shakes his head. "There are poachers who kill gorillas. Sometimes they say they needed money for their family. But poachers are very selfish. They take something that belongs to everyone and take the money for themselves. We have very few gorillas. The money the government gets from gorilla tourists pays for schools and hospitals. Some people say, 'Oh, the government thinks gorillas are more important than people.' That is not true. And we should remember that the gorillas have a right to be there."

Innocent asks, "Would you all like to see a gorilla someday?" He grins as every hand goes up in the air.

After thanking the students, Innocent leaves Seseme Primary School. He is on his way to visit mountain gorillas. But Innocent makes one more stop. Ntungamo Primary School sits on a ridge overlooking Bwindi Impenetrable Forest. Unlike the students at Seseme, these students know gorillas very well.

"How many of you have seen a gorilla?" asks Innocent. Most of the children raise their hand.

"I've seen them in our garden," a girl tells Innocent.

"Sometimes they eat our crops," adds a boy.

ABOVE: Juvenile gorillas can feed themselves. But they still need their gorilla family for safety, warmth, and comfort.

FACING PAGE: The children at this Ugandan school live close to mountain gorillas. You can see the tree-covered hills of Bwindi Impenetrable Forest in the background.

Most of the children have seen a mountain gorilla—sometimes right in their own backyard!

Innocent quizzes them. They know all the answers: the mountain gorilla lives only in Uganda, Rwanda, and the Democratic Republic of the Congo. Mountain gorillas live in groups led by a silverback. The gorillas eat plants (unfortunately, sometimes from gardens). The gorillas act a lot like people.

Innocent learns something, too. The money for two new schoolrooms under construction at Ntungamo comes from gorilla tourism.

"Who likes gorillas?" Innocent asks. He isn't exactly sure of their answer. After all, these gorillas can be a real problem. You can't chase a gorilla out of your garden like you can a rabbit.

The children smile. Every hand goes up.

Good news! A recent census found that there are now about 720 mountain gorillas. In 1989 there were only about 625.

Helping the Gorillas

Just by reading this book, you are helping mountain gorillas. Half of the royalties from *Gorilla Doctors: Saving Endangered Great Apes* are donated to the Mountain Gorilla Veterinary Project. You can visit the project online at http://mgvp.32ad.com.

Postscript

Maisha (left) plays with Fearless (right).

Fearless is now about six years old. He lives in a special orphan care facility in Rwanda. Unfortunately, other baby gorillas have been orphaned in recent years, and MGVP veterinarians (with the help of the Dian Fossey Gorilla Fund International, the Rwandan Tourism and National Parks Office, and the Congolese Institute for Nature Conservation) are now caring for ten young gorillas.

The first new orphan Fearless met was Maisha, a female mountain gorilla about the same age as him. Despite his name, at first Fearless was intimidated by the energetic Maisha. Now they are good friends. Fearless did bond instantly with one-year-old Dunia. Like Fearless, Dunia is an eastern lowland gorilla. Police rescued Dunia from poachers who had kept the terrified baby zipped up in a duffel bag. Felicia's husband, the gorilla vet Chris Whittier, reports that at the end of their first meeting "Dunia had to be pried from Fearless's thick mitts as he was unwilling to give up the little sweetheart."

Fearless, Maisha, and Dunia and the seven other young gorillas (four eastern lowland and three mountain gorillas) being cared for by MGVP and their partners were confiscated from poachers. One young gorilla was found with a severe hand injury; the vets were forced to amputate the hand. Another orphan was rescued after its parents were found shot to death in the forest.

The MGVP scientists believe that by being raised together these young gorillas will develop gorilla social skills and behaviors like wild-raised gorillas. Eventually, they hope all of the orphaned gorillas will be able to return home—into the wild, where they belong.

ACKNOWLEDGMENTS

The best part of writing a Scientists in the Field book is going into the field (in this case, forest) with scientists like Dr. Lynne Gaffikin, Dr. Mike Cranfield, Dr. Innocent Rwego, and Dr. Felicia Nutter. I am most grateful to them for their patient explanations and good company. I would also like to thank Dr. Chris Whittier and Jospin Ngubiri Mbonekube of MGVP; Dr. Robert Hilsenroth and Carissa Lester of the Morris Animal Foundation; Dr. Arthur Mugisha and Silver

Mbonigaba of the Uganda Wildlife Authority; Patience Dusabimana, Francois Bigirimana, and Elisabeth Nyirakaragire of the Office Rwandaise du Tourisme et des Parc Nationaux; Jean-Paul Gahire of the Karisoke Research Center; Godfrey Muramira and the students of Seseme Primary School; Abel Maniragaba and the students of Ntungamo Primary School; Dr. George Schaller of the Wildlife Conservation Society; Markye Gray of the International Gorilla Conservation Program; Dr. Gladys Kalema-Zikusoka of Conservation Through Public Health; and Alecia Lilly of the Dian Fossey Gorilla Fund International. Special thanks to my editor, Hannah Rodgers, and to book designers Lisa Diercks and Gabrielle Cosel.

Resources

BOOKS

Fossey, Dian. *Gorillas in the Mist* (Boston: Houghton Mifflin, 1983).

Nichols, Michael, and George B. Schaller. *Gorilla: Struggle for Survival in the Virungas* (New York: Aperture Foundation, 1989).

Matthews, Tom L. *Light Shining Through the Mist: A Photobiography of Dian Fossey* (Washington, D.C.: National Geographic Society, 1998).

Redmond, Ian. *Eyewitness Guides: Gorilla* (London: Dorling Kindersley, 2000).

OTHER GORILLA CONSERVATION WEB SITES

Dian Fossey Gorilla Fund International: www.gorillafund.org

International Gorilla Conservation Program: www.mountaingorillas.org

The Great Ape Survival Project: www.unep.org/grasp/

Fearless gives Dunia a hug.

Index

PHOTO CREDITS:

•Carl Akeley/American Museum of Natural History: p. 14

•Paul Blumenthal: p. 45

•Robert I.M. Campbell/National Geographic Image Collection: p. 16

•Mike Cranfield/MGVP: pp. 1, 7

•Lynne Gaffikin: pp. 28, 59

•Maryke Gray/IGCP: pp. 6, 8, 9, 10, 11

•Copyright 2004 Lisa Hoffner/ Wild-Eye Photography: pp. 2, 44(top)

•Dr. Gladys Kalema-Zikusoka: p. 33

•George B. Schaller: p. 15

•Pamela S. Turner: pp. 4, 12, 17, 22, 27, 30, 32, 34, 36, 40, 43, 48–54, 56–58

•Chris Whittier: pp. 20, 21, 37, 38, 41, 42, 45, 61–63

•Chris Whittier/MGVP/DFGFI: pp. 24, 26, 44(bottom)

Book design by Lisa Diercks
The text of this book is set in The Mix.

Library of Congress Cataloging-in-Publication Data

Turner, Pamela S.
  Gorilla doctors : saving endangered great apes / by Pamela S. Turner.
    p. cm.
  PA ISBN-13: 978-0-547-01433-3
  HC ISBN-13: 978-0-618-44555-4
1. Gorilla—Wounds and injuries—Rwanda—Parc national des volcans. 2. Gorilla—Diseases—Rwanda—Parc national des volcans. 3. Wildlife veterinarians—Rwanda—Parc national des volcans. 4. Parc national des volcans (Rwanda). I. Title.
  SF997.5.G65T87 2005
  333.95'988416'096751—dc22
  2004009213

Printed in China
22 SCP 20 19 18 17 16 15 14 13